Native Americans of the Eastern Woodlands

BY DAVID BOWMAN

Table of Contents

Introduction

The Eastern Woodlands Indians lived in the eastern part of the United States. They lived in a huge area that stretched from the Atlantic Ocean to the Mississippi River. The St. Lawrence River formed the northern border of their land. The southern border was what is now North Carolina.

The Indians belonged to **tribes**. A tribe is a group of people who have the same **ancestors** and way of living. Many tribes spoke the same language, but not all of them did. Two of the language groups were Iroquoian (eer-uh-KWOY-uhn) and Algonquian (ahl-GAHN-kwee-uhn).

This engraving ▶ shows a tribe settlement in New York.

2

In this book, you will learn about three of the Eastern Woodlands tribes: the Iroquois (EER-uh-kwoy), the Cherokee (CHAIR-uh-kee), and the Shawnee (shaw-NEE). The Iroquois and the Cherokee spoke Iroquoian. The Shawnee spoke Algonquian. You will see how these tribes lived long ago. You will learn what their daily lives were like. You will visit where they live today. And you will also see their **customs** and traditions from the past and from today. Let's meet the Native Americans of the Eastern Woodlands.

Traditional
Ways of Life

The Eastern Woodlands tribes lived in many different **environments**. Some tribes lived in the mountains. Some lived by rivers. Some tribes lived in the forest. Each area had very different **climates**.

The Iroquois lived near the Great Lakes. It is very cold in winter and hot in summer there. The Shawnee lived in the Ohio River Valley, which has a similar climate. The Cherokee

▲ The tribes fished and hunted near where they lived.

used to live around the Great Lakes. Then, in the 1500s, they lost their land in battle. They were forced to move. The Cherokee moved near the Appalachian Mountains. The land there is very rocky. Each tribe **adapted**, or changed, their lifestyle to suit the place where they lived.

Most Eastern Woodlands Indian tribes settled near water. Plants and animals are most often found near water. The Eastern Woodlands Indians depended on them for food.

1. SOLVE THIS

Look at the map and locate the three tribes. About how far did they live from one another? Use the map scale and a ruler to figure it out. Round distances to the nearest whole number. Then answer the following:

a. About how far did the Cherokee live from the Shawnee?

b. About how far did the Shawnee live from the Iroquois?

c. About how far were the Iroquois from the Cherokee?

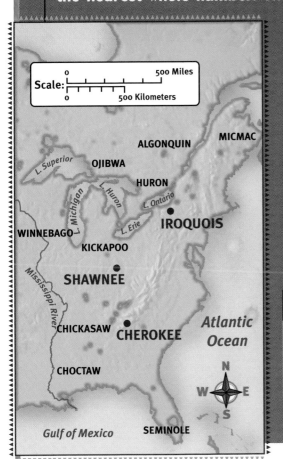

Math ✔ Point

Do your answers make sense? Why or why not?

No Place Like Home

Most Eastern Woodlands Indians lived in **wigwams** or **longhouses**. The Shawnee lived in wigwams. They bent young tree branches into a dome shape. They left a hole at the side of the wigwam for a door. They made another hole at the top of the wigwam. It let smoke from their cooking fires escape. Only one family lived in each wigwam.

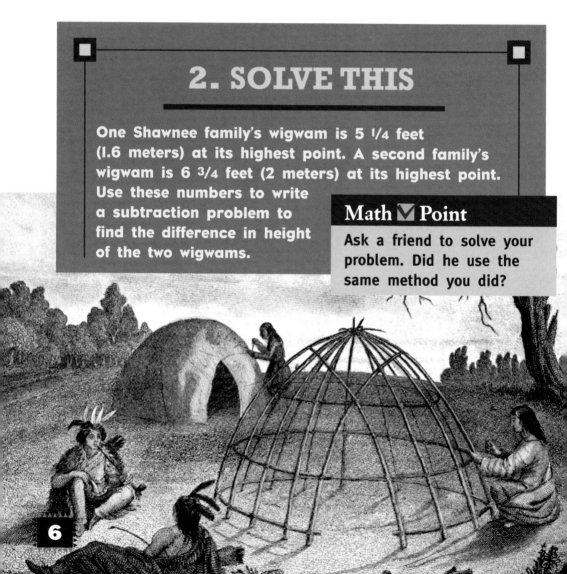

2. SOLVE THIS

One Shawnee family's wigwam is 5 1/4 feet (1.6 meters) at its highest point. A second family's wigwam is 6 3/4 feet (2 meters) at its highest point. Use these numbers to write a subtraction problem to find the difference in height of the two wigwams.

Math ✓ Point

Ask a friend to solve your problem. Did he use the same method you did?

The Iroquois and the Cherokee usually lived in longhouses. Longhouses were long, rectangular homes. They were made from small trees. They were covered with pieces of bark that had been sewn together. Many families lived in one longhouse. Longhouses were like apartments.

Here are some everyday objects that you would have found in a wigwam or a longhouse:

◀**Pots.** Women made pots out of clay. They used them for cooking, carrying water from a nearby lake or stream, and storing food. Dishes, plates, and spoons were made from tree bark.

◀**Mortar and Pestle.** Indians put corn or other vegetables in a mortar, a kind of bowl. Then they ground it up with a pestle, a kind of stick. The mortar and pestle were made from stone. They needed to be strong.

◀**Central Fireplace.** The fire inside the house kept everyone warm. The Indians cooked there if the weather was cold or rainy.

◀**Sleeping Platform.** The Indians slept on hard wooden platforms raised off the ground. They stored tools and supplies under their beds.

In the Garden

Most Eastern Woodlands Indians had gardens outside their homes. To make a garden, the men first cleared away rocks and plants from a patch of ground. Then the women planted seeds. They built up little mounds of dirt. They planted a few kernels of corn in the center of each mound. Around the corn, they planted beans and squash. As the beans grew, they wrapped around the cornstalk. It gave them support from the wind and rain. The Indians discovered that if they buried some dead fish in the soil, the ground would produce better crops. Most children helped the women take care of the garden. They watered and weeded the plants.

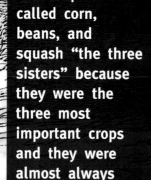

IT'S A FACT

The Iroquois called corn, beans, and squash "the three sisters" because they were the three most important crops and they were almost always planted together.

▲ Everyone in the family worked in the garden.

On the Hunt

The Eastern Woodlands Indians also hunted for food. They hunted deer, bears, and rabbits. They used bows and arrows or spears to kill the animals. They ate the meat and made the skins into clothing and other things.

The Indians also fished from canoes that they made. They often caught fish in nets made from strong branches.

▲ The Indians used every part of the animals they killed. They even made spoons and fishhooks out of the bones.

Historical Perspective

The food that people eat can tell you a lot about them. You can learn what kinds of plants and animals lived near them. You can find out how they cooked. You might even discover clues about their health. The Eastern Woodlands Indians had many tasty recipes for teas, breads, puddings, meat, fish, vegetables, and other things. Of course, they didn't have many foods that we eat today. Can you think of reasons why not?

Clothes from Nature

Eastern Woodlands Indians used the plants and animals around them to make clothing. Many plants could be dried out and then woven into a kind of cloth. Animal skins could be made into furs and leather.

The Shawnee and the Cherokee wore similar clothing. Women wore grass skirts over leggings made from animal hides. The men wore pieces of animal skin around their waists called breechcloth. This served as underwear. Then, if it was cold, they tied on pant legs made from leather and a cape or robe of animal skin or fur. Men and women wore moccasins on their feet.

▲ Clothing was often made of animal hides.

For ceremonies or in times of war, the men of the Eastern Woodlands tribes often painted designs on their faces. They also wore beaded headbands with feathers in them. Often, men tattooed their bodies to celebrate winning a battle.

▲ The Iroquois wore warm clothing because of the cold climate in which they lived.

The Iroquois, who lived in a colder climate, wore shirts, leggings, and moccasins made of **buckskin**, which is a soft hide made from the skin of a deer. Tribe leaders often wore robes and headdresses made of feathers and fur. Women wore skirts woven out of wild grass. They covered themselves in furs. Most of the time, children did not wear any clothing at all.

IT'S A FACT

The most respected Eastern Woodlands Indian warriors and elder tribesmen wore silver nose rings and earrings. Men cut slits into their ears and wrapped the skin in silver wire. The weight of the wire stretched the skin into great holes. The larger the holes, the more respected these men were.

11

Families and Communities

Families played an important role for the Eastern Woodlands Indians. Each family belonged to a **clan**. A clan is a group of families that has the same ancestors. A tribe was made up of many clans.

In Iroquoian tribes, such as the Cherokee and Iroquois, power was passed down on the female side of the family. An elder woman headed each clan. She was known as the clan mother. Clan mothers owned the crops and houses. They had great power. They had final say over everything the tribe did. Clan mothers usually worked together to elect chiefs of each of the tribes. Algonquin tribes like the Shawnee, however, had clan fathers. Power passed through the men.

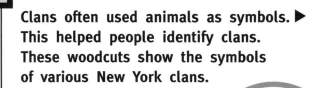

Clans often used animals as symbols. ▶
This helped people identify clans.
These woodcuts show the symbols
of various New York clans.

Working Together

Many tribes in the Northeast formed **confederacies** (kuhn-FEH-duh-ruh-seez). Confederacies were groups of tribes that worked together. Some confederacies had great power. The largest and most powerful of these was the Iroquois Confederacy. It was also called the League of Five Nations. The Iroquois Confederacy was made up of five tribes—the Mohawk, Onondaga, Oneida, Cayuga, and Seneca. It passed laws and worked much like the United States government does today.

With the start of the Iroquois Confederacy, all tribes that spoke the Iroquoian language came to be known as Iroquois. In time, even the Cherokee were mainly known as an Iroquois tribe.

They Made a Difference

According to one legend, Deganawidah (day-gah-nuh-WEE-duh) was the founder of the Iroquois Confederacy. He convinced the Mohawk chief Hiawatha to end war with neighboring tribes and establish peace. Deganawidah set down the Great Law of Peace. He chose the white pine tree as the symbol of the Great Law of Peace. Under this tree, all weapons of war would be buried. At the top sat an eagle to guard the peace.

▼ Members of the tribes that make up the Iroquois Confederacy still meet today.

13

Party Time

The Native Americans of the Eastern Woodlands had many festivals and celebrations during the year. Many are still celebrated today.

The most popular Cherokee celebration was the Corn Festival. It honored the planting and harvesting of corn. At the Corn Festival, people painted their faces white to show happiness.

The Cherokee loved to play games at their festivals. A favorite game was called Chunkey. The Cherokee made a flat disc out of a finely ground stone. They rolled the disc across a smooth surface. Two players carrying long poles would run after the disc and throw poles at it. The person whose pole landed closest to where the disc stopped won points.

The Shawnee were well known for their storytelling skills. They loved to tell tales and legends about their ancestors. These stories were passed from generation to generation. Many of the tales are still told today.

Cherokee ▶ dancers in their native costume at a National Indian Festival

14

POINT

Read More About It
Ask your teacher or librarian to help you find books and Internet sites where you can learn about other games the Cherokee enjoyed, such as lacrosse.

The Sacred Bowl Game

The Iroquois celebrated the Ceremony of Midwinter every January or February. This was in honor of the first new moon after the longest night of the year. On the last day of the ceremony, they played the Sacred Bowl Game.

▲ playing the sacred bowl game

To play this game, the Iroquois decorated a wooden bowl with four clan symbols—the bear, wolf, turtle, and deer. A player put six nuts inside the bowl and hit the bowl against the ground. If five of the six nuts landed on the same symbol, the player scored one point and took another turn. The first player to reach ten points won the game.

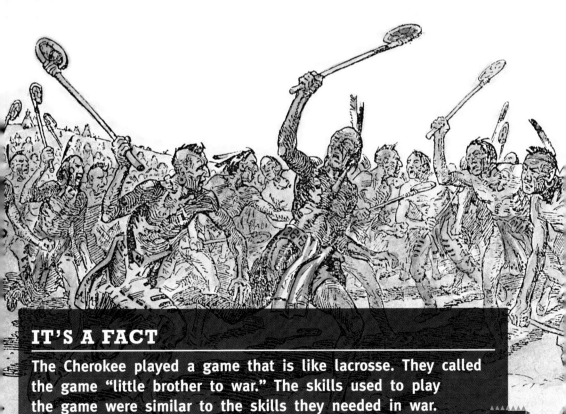

IT'S A FACT

The Cherokee played a game that is like lacrosse. They called the game "little brother to war." The skills used to play the game were similar to the skills they needed in war. The game improved their coordination and war skills.

Chapter 2

Changes
and Challenges

The Eastern Woodlands Indians were among the first tribes to meet and live with Europeans. The two cultures learned from each other. The Europeans had metal tools and weapons. The Indians already had copper, but iron and steel were new to them. They quickly realized that metal knives, fishhooks, and kettles worked better. Metal knives cut faster and better. Metal fishhooks and kettles lasted longer. Europeans also had guns. The Indians saw that guns would help them hunt and defend themselves better.

▲ Metal tools improved the Indians' lives.

The Native Americans had many things that the Europeans liked and wanted, too. The Europeans were very interested in furs. They especially wanted beaver fur. Hats covered with beaver fur were very popular in Europe. The tribes taught the Europeans how to hunt and trap animals for fur.

The Indians knew a great deal about North American soil, climate, and crops. They taught the Europeans how to hunt and fish. They also passed on their farming methods. They taught the Europeans how to fertilize the soil to grow more food. At first, the Indians and the Europeans got along peacefully. Each learned from the other.

IT'S A FACT

Europeans brought beads to trade with the Indians. The Indians used these beads for jewelry and as gifts on special occasions. Their name for the beads was wampum.

◀ The Indians knew many different ways to grow crops and store food. This helped the Europeans survive during the cold winters.

Losing People

The early settlers brought many useful things with them. They also brought diseases. Many of these diseases had not existed in America before the settlers came. The Indians had never before suffered from mumps, measles, or smallpox. Therefore, their bodies could not fight off these diseases. Most of the Indians who got sick died.

So the number of Native Americans grew smaller. At the same time, more and more settlers were coming to the United States. They began to want the Indians' lands. Soon, the two groups began to fight over land.

3. SOLVE THIS

When the first Europeans arrived, there were about 50,000 Cherokee people. Smallpox cut the number by 50%. Then the American Revolution killed another 50% of the remaining Cherokee people. About how many Cherokee were left after the American Revolution?

Math ☑ Point

How could you check your answer?

▲ This woodcut shows Indians in Massachusetts in the 1600s dying of smallpox.

THEY MADE A DIFFERENCE

Sequoyah (sih-KWOY-uh) was born in 1776. He is famous for developing the Cherokee alphabet. He fled Tennessee as a child when white settlers arrived. After the American Revolution, he began to create a writing system. He called it the "Talking Leaves." The system is made up of eighty-five letters.

In 1821, the Cherokee Nation adopted Sequoyah's alphabet as their own. Within months, thousands of Cherokee learned to read and write. The Europeans could not read Talking Leaves and had no idea what the Cherokee were writing about.

D a	R e	T i	Ꮊ o	Ꮎ u	i v
Ꮝ ga Ꭴ ka	Ꮆ ge	Ᏼ gi	A go	J gu	E gv
Ꮂ ha	Ꮅ he	Ꮥ hi	Ꮄ ho	Ꮁ hu	Ꮧ hv
W la	Ꮣ le	Ꮅ li	Ꮐ lo	M lu	Ꮑ lv
Ꮉ ma	Ꮨ me	H mi	Ꮒ mo	Ꮠ mu	
Ꮎ na Ꮏ hna Ꮇ nah	Ꮮ ne	Ꮒ ni	Z no	Ꮔ nu	Ꮕ nv
Ꮖ qua	Ꮗ que	Ꮕ qui	Ꮘ quo	Ꮘ quu	Ꮙ quv
Ꮚ sa Ꮝ s	Ꮞ se	Ꮏ si	Ꮟ so	Ꮡ su	R sv
Ꮫ da Ꮤ ta	Ꮝ de Ꮦ te	Ꮧ di Ꮨ ti	V do	Ꮪ du	Ꮫ dv
Ꮬ dla Ꮯ tla	L tle	C tli	Ꮰ tlo	Ꮰ tlu	P tlv
Ꮳ tsa	Ꮴ tse	Ꮧ tsi	K tso	Ꮫ tsu	Ꮴ tsv
G wa	Ꮺ we	Ꮝ wi	Ꮼ wo	Ꮽ wu	6 wv
Ꮿ ya	Ᏼ ye	Ꮈ yi	Ꮧ yo	Ꮐ yu	B yv

▲ Sequoyah's Talking Leaves is one of the few original alphabets in the world.

Losing Land

The Cherokee were able to hold on to their land for many years after the American Revolution. Most other tribes had been forced to go west. They settled on lands set aside for them called reservations. But finally, in 1830, the U.S. Congress passed the Indian Removal Act. This act forced the Cherokee and other tribes off their land. Nearly 100,000 people from many Eastern Woodlands tribes were forced to move west. In 1838 and 1839, their bitter journey on foot caused so much sickness and death that it is known today as the Trail of Tears.

In the years after the Trail of Tears, Indian tribes all over North America lost more and more land. The United States wanted the Indians to become farmers in the West. So, in 1887, the General Dawes Allotment Act was passed. It gave reservation land to individual Native Americans, but most Native Americans did not know how to farm. They had no farming equipment and no seeds.

By the early 1900s, Native American life in the Eastern Woodlands had all but disappeared. A few small reservations still existed there, but life on reservations everywhere was hard. Tribes had been separated. Families and clans had been split up. The Iroquois Confederacy was no longer able to meet. The United States tried to change the Native American way of life. They wanted the Indians to live like the settlers did.

IT'S A FACT

In the late 1800s, many Indian children were taken from their families and sent to boarding school. There, Indian children were taught the customs and way of life of the European culture.

A New
Beginning

By 1900, things began to change for Native Americans. The United States government began to grant rights to Native Americans. It began to return some of the land that had been taken from the Native Americans. Here are some important events for Native Americans that took place after 1900.

1924 In the Snyder Act, the United States government granted American citizenship to all Native Americans.

1934 In the Indian Reorganization Act, the U.S. government distributed land to tribes instead of individuals. It gave them the power to create their own governments and manage their own people. The Cherokee (Iroquois) and Shawnee were given land in Oklahoma to be shared with more than twenty-five other tribes.

1946 The U.S. government set up an Indian Claims Commission. This group was created so that tribes could get payment from the U.S. government for land that was taken. This same year, the U.S. government paid the Cherokee Nation $15 million for land it took.

1969–1971 A group of Native Americans formed the American Indian Movement (AIM). Members of Indian tribes from all over the United States took over Alcatraz Island in San Francisco Bay. They lived in the old prison for nearly two years.

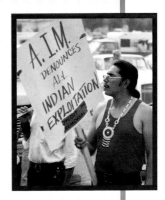

4. SOLVE THIS

The American Revolution ended in 1783. Many Eastern Woodlands tribes were forced off their land then. How many years were there between the end of the Revolution and the date of each of the events in the time line?

Math ☑ Point

Are your answers reasonable? Why or why not?

Where Are They Now?

Today, most of the Eastern Woodlands Indian tribes live on reservations, but they do not live in the Eastern Woodlands. The Cherokee once lived in parts of Tennessee, North Carolina, South Carolina, Mississippi, Alabama, and Virginia. Today, they live on reservations in Oklahoma with more than twenty-five other tribes. The Shawnee used to live in what is now Ohio. Today, they also live on a reservation in Oklahoma. Most Iroquoian tribes now live in California and Oklahoma.

▼ These Eastern Woodlands Indians now live in Oklahoma.

✓ POINT

Visualize

Imagine that you live on a reservation in Oklahoma or California. How do you feel the first time you hear the story of your ancestors? How will you honor your heritage?

Native American Government

Each tribe now has its own government. The tribes vote for their own laws. They elect their own leaders. They pay taxes to their own reservations. There are 562 tribal governments in the United States, but their power only applies on their own land. Outside reservations, Native Americans are full citizens of the United States. They vote in U.S. elections.

The U.S. Bureau of Indian Affairs oversees these tribal governments. It takes care of reservation land and forests. It makes sure the tribes have basic services. The Bureau also provides money for education to more than 48,000 Native American students in the United States.

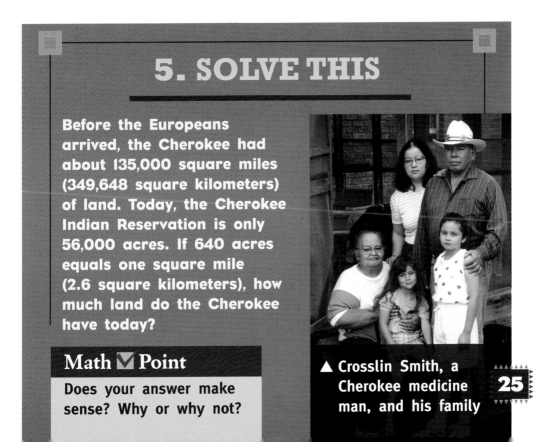

5. SOLVE THIS

Before the Europeans arrived, the Cherokee had about 135,000 square miles (349,648 square kilometers) of land. Today, the Cherokee Indian Reservation is only 56,000 acres. If 640 acres equals one square mile (2.6 square kilometers), how much land do the Cherokee have today?

Math ☑ Point

Does your answer make sense? Why or why not?

▲ Crosslin Smith, a Cherokee medicine man, and his family

25

It's Art

Eastern Woodlands Indian tribes have always been known for their arts and crafts skills. Today, the pots and bowls they made long ago to hold food and water are admired for their beauty. Museums put them on display. Art stores sell them. Many of the traditional crafts that Eastern Woodlands tribes used long ago are still in use today.

◀ **Dreamcatchers.** Native American tribes believed that a dreamcatcher kept bad dreams away by catching them in a net. Dreamcatchers are said to bring good luck and keep evil spirits away.

◀ **Painted Hides.** Native Americans once painted famous battles or events in history on animal skins. These beautiful paintings are works of art.

◀ **Drums.** Native American tribes still use drums like this one during ceremonies and festivals. Most drums are made by hand using natural materials.

CAREERS

Today, the members of Eastern Woodlands tribes belong to every kind of profession and do every kind of job. Doctors, dentists, paramedics, and nurses are almost always in demand on Indian reservations. Reservations have their own hospitals and medical offices. They also need teachers for their schools and forest rangers to help protect the land. Native Americans also work at the Bureau of Indian Affairs as firemen, park rangers, chefs, accountants, and pharmacists.

Wilma Mankiller, principle chief of the Cherokee Nation, on the Cherokee Indian Reservation in Oklahoma

Conclusion

The Eastern Woodlands Indians lived off the land for thousands of years. Then the first European settlers arrived. The Europeans brought guns, cooking utensils, and many other things that the Indians wanted. But the settlers also brought diseases. Many Indians got sick and died. The settlers also wanted more and more land. Wars broke out. Many tribes lost more than half of their members to war and disease.

dancing at ▶
a powwow

During the 1800s and 1900s, the Eastern Woodlands tribes were forced off their land. They moved west. The move did great harm to their families and communities. Children were sent to boarding schools. Many Native Americans led very hard lives.

But then things got better. Native Americans were made U.S. citizens. They won the right to vote. Today, reservations around the United States have their own governments. They have their own laws. Native American arts, crafts, and customs are still alive and well today. Many Native Americans enjoy sharing their customs and traditions with all Americans.

 Important Events for Native Americans

1400s	Iroquois Confederacy formed
1776	**Sequoyah born**
1821	Cherokee Nation adopts Sequoyah's alphabet
1830	**Indian Removal Act**
1838–1839	Trail of Tears
1887	**General Dawes Allotment Act**
1924	Snyder Act
1934	**Indian Reorganization Act**
1946	Indian Claims Commission set up
1969–71	**American Indian Movement (AIM) formed**

Solve This Answers

1. Page 5
   a. The Cherokee were about 300 miles (482.8 kilometers) from the Shawnee.
   b. The Shawnee were about 400 miles (643.7 kilometers) from the Iroquois.
   c. The Iroquois were about 650 miles (1,046.1 kilometers) from the Cherokee.

2. Page 6
   6 3/4 feet – 5 1/4 feet = 1 2/4 feet or 1 1/2 feet
   (2 meters – 1.6 meters = .4 meters)

3. Page 18
   Cherokee people surviving the smallpox outbreak:
   50% of 50,000 = 0.50 x 50,000 or 1/2 x 50,000 = 25,000 Cherokee people survived the smallpox outbreak.
   Cherokee people surviving the American Revolution:
   50% of 25,000 = 0.5 x 25,000 or 1/2 x 25,000 = 12,500 Cherokee people survived the American Revolution.

4. Page 23
   a. Snyder Act: 1924 – 1783 = 141 years
   b. Indian Reorganization Act: 1934 – 1783 = 151 years
   c. Indian Claims Commission: 1946 – 1783 = 163 years
   d. American Indian Movement:
      1969 – 1783 = 186 years
      1971 – 1783 = 188 years

5. Page 25
   $$\frac{56{,}000 \text{ acres} \times 1 \text{ square mile}}{640 \text{ acres}} = 87.5 \text{ square miles}$$

   $$\frac{56{,}000 \text{ acres} \times 2.6 \text{ square km}}{640 \text{ acres}} = 227.5 \text{ square km}$$

Glossary

adapt   (uh-DAPT) to change in order to survive (page 4)

ancestor   (AN-sehs-tuhr) a person from whom one is descended (page 2)

buckskin   (BUHK-skihn) a strong, soft, tan leather made from the skin of deer (page 11)

clan   (KLAN) a group of families descended from the same ancestors (page 12)

climate   (KLY-miht) the temperature, wind, and weather conditions of a particular area of land (page 4)

confederacy   (kuhn-FEH-duh-ruh-see) a group of tribes that worked together (page 13)

custom   (KUHS-tuhm) a tradition; a way of life (page 3)

environment   (ihn-VY-ruhn-mehnt) the air, the water, the soil, and all the other things that surround a person, animal, or plant (page 4)

longhouse   (LAWNG-hows) a long dwelling built of poles and bark, shared by a number of families (page 6)

tribe   (TRYB) a group of people who have the same ancestors and way of living (page 2)

wigwam   (WIHG-wahm) a hut made of poles covered with bark, leaves, or hides (page 6)

Index